Joel Benton, William Sloane Kennedy

Emerson as a Poet

Joel Benton, William Sloane Kennedy

Emerson as a Poet

ISBN/EAN: 9783743383449

Manufactured in Europe, USA, Canada, Australia, Japa

Cover: Foto ©Thomas Meinert / pixelio.de

Manufactured and distributed by brebook publishing software
(www.brebook.com)

Joel Benton, William Sloane Kennedy

Emerson as a Poet

EMERSON AS A POET

BY

JOEL BENTON

Rien de ce qui ne transporte pas n'est poésie.
La lyre est un instrument ailé.—*Joubert.*

NEW-YORK
M. L. HOLBROOK & CO.
1882

Wenn des Dichters Mühle geht,
Halte sie nicht ein!
Denn wer einmal uns versteht,
Wird uns auch verzeihn.

                                        Goethe.

The words of a good poet, even when we do not apprehend their full meaning, pour a stream of sweet nectar upon the soul.

From the Hindu of the Sarngadhara Paddhati.

There is, indeed, a certain low and moderate sort of poetry that a man may well enough judge by certain rules of art; but the true, supreme, and divine Poesy is above all the rules of reason. Whoever discovers the beauty of it, with the most assured and most steady sight, sees no more than the quick reflection of a flash of lightning. This is a sort of poetry that does not exercise, but ravishes and overwhelms our judgment.

                                        Montaigne.

Dedication.

TO

WALTER H. POMEROY,

WHOSE EARLY AND
CONSTANT APPRECIATION OF
EMERSON AND OF THE HIGHEST
MINDS MAKES THIS ASSOCIATION APT, EVEN
IF HALF A LIFE-TIME OF GENEROUS FRIEND-
SHIP WERE NOT ALSO IN THE SCALE, I
DEDICATE, WITH ESPECIAL PLEAS-
URE, THIS LITTLE
VOLUME.

J. B.

PREFATORY NOTE.

*I*T *seems necessary to say that this essay was written over a year and a half ago, and is given here substantially in the form that it then had. No essential change has been made to accommodate it to Mr. Emerson's death, or to do justice to the multitude of sayings that this event elicited. If but little has been added, a few points have been slightly expanded while preparing it for the press. The portion read at Concord, on the day set apart to Emerson by the "School of Philosophy," was a fragment, only a brief synopsis of which was furnished for the book representing the lectures of that body.*

For the privilege of copying so liberally from Mr. Emerson's poems, I am indebted to the courtesy of Messrs. Houghton, Mifflin & Co.; and to Mr. C. H. Brainard, of Washington, for the right to reduce for an appropriate frontispiece the admirable lithograph of Emerson, which had its origin in a photograph owned by Theodore Parker, and which was Mr. Parker's favorite picture of this author. To many others, also, no other portrait of Emerson recalls him so perfectly in his best attitude, as he was in his prime.

I am sure, whatever judgment this essay may provoke, that the addition of Mr. Kennedy's Concordance to Mr. Emerson's poetry, which he has kindly permitted me to make, will prove a welcome feature in this offering.

J. B.

Amenia, N. Y., Oct. 5, 1882.

CONTENTS.

MR. EMERSON AS A POET.

I hold it of little matter
Whether your jewel be of pure water,
A rose diamond or a white,
But whether it dazzle me with light.
EMERSON.

Charm is the glory which makes
Song of the poet divine.
MATTHEW ARNOLD.

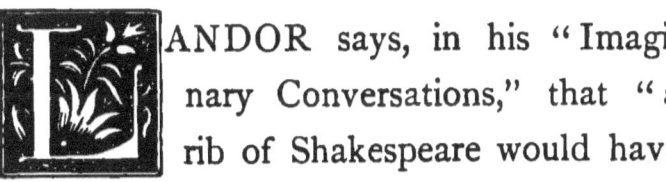ANDOR says, in his "Imagi-
nary Conversations," that "a
rib of Shakespeare would have
made Milton—the same portion of Milton,
all poets born ever since." Something
of this largeness and intensity—this su-
premacy of genius—belongs to Emerson.

So dense and pervading is his peculiar and individual force, it might, if properly distributed, be made to equip and light a literary constellation. We must go back to Shakespeare and Milton, among English names, to find an equally enormous endowment. If it does not stream in versatility, it towers in commanding altitude.* Among his contemporaries we may name, to be sure, notable men of a more composite order— but no personality at once so compact, so essence-like, so opulent, so strong. While his power is well authenticated in one direction by all who are competent to speak of it, it is curious, and not quite explicable, that the current literary criticism conspires to go so completely around his poetry. It leaves it, indeed, in almost

* Dr. Bartol says : " If Shakespeare or Goethe be the Mont Blanc, Emerson is a neighboring Aiguille of lesser breadth, but well-nigh equal height."

solitary neglect—surrounds it as if, among the high products of literary expression in this century, it alone should be reserved as an island for silence. Let us admit at the outset, if you will, that the fortitude of his strain—as Matthew Arnold says of the verses of Epictetus—"is for the strong, for the few; even for them the spiritual atmosphere with which it surrounds them is bleak and gray"—and that

> "The solemn peaks but to the stars are known,
> But to the stars and the cold lunar beams;
> Alone the sun arises, and alone
>   Spring the great streams."

But, the best minds concede the brilliancy of Emerson's thought, and find delight in its acuteness and depth. They accept his power in prose,—and this prose, unmatchable and radiant, is itself better poetry than the verses of many reputable singers. They do not refuse to rate him

as a philosopher, and almost as a prophet;
but, so far as concerns any adequate statement, they overlook and pass by his over-
whelming preponderance as a poet. There
are those who think Carlyle's often expressed and notorious dislike of modern
verse-making (does this spring from his
own failure to succeed in it?), resulting in
certain proffered advice, and joined with
Emerson's almost maiden modesty as an
aspirant, led the latter some time since
into the habit * of disparaging his own great
gift. So that we have the singular phe-
nomenon of the author of the most pure,
aërial and divinely souled poetry since
Shakespeare's music became measured and
still, and the literary world together, fall-

* An anecdote, giving some pleasant badinage
between Emerson and an interviewer on this
point, is gracefully told by a writer in *Scribner's
Monthly* for February, 1880.

ing into a condition of mind which, except casually and fragmentarily, ignores its validity and almost disputes its existence. But can it be believed that Shakespeare inwardly did not know he was Shakespeare, or that Emerson was really in doubt about his own marvelous vision and melody?

I purpose, in a brief paper, not by any means to make up the deficiency I lament, but to offer a few cursory suggestions which may prompt others who have the truth in view, and the requisite fitness, to show the courage of their convictions on this subject.

One need not go far, of course, to see why Emerson's poetry is not accepted and popular in the way that Longfellow's or Whittier's is; for he does not aim to mediate to the average mind, and will not address the careless and irresolute thought. He shuns the dramatic form,—omits the shining thread of narrative,—and cannot stoop to tickle an ephemeral and idle fancy. These things are well to do, and honorable in their sphere; but, apart from, and above them, there should be ample room to furnish him a well-recognized seat in the modern Parnassus. May he not at least be placed along with Browning, even if the latter does transform the world into a stage and play-house? If you call his style obscure, how will you characterize Browning's? I will not say, take for an example this last writer's " Sordello," which was recalled and rewritten to make it apprehensible; but take " The Ring and the Book "—take the most famous poems, and the most of the verse he has written, extended or brief (excepting " Evelyn Hope " and " The Pied Piper of Hamelin "),—and what does the average reader make of them? But Browning, in spite of thick obscurity, and what seems latterly like intolerable affectation, enters into large account with all writers who attempt to deal with English poetry; he is marked and measured, a society is formed around his name, and he has the unmistakable distinction of having caused reams of paper to be written over with most careful praise or the most complimentary fault-finding. Who has yet sounded the true note in respect to Emerson's poems? Who, in fact, has considered them with any thoughtful or elaborate attention? Casual notice, of course, they have received; but, in the main, the critics, in consideration of his permitted prose and unimpeachable moral flavor, have simply condescended, in silence, to forgive him for being a poet.

Very likely Emerson can say, as Browning is lately attributed with saying to a friend: " I can have little doubt that my writing has been in the main too hard for many I should have been pleased to communicate with; but I never designedly tried to puzzle people, as some of my critics have supposed. On the other hand, I never pretended to offer such literature as should be a substitute for a cigar or a game of dominoes to an idle man."

I must make a memorandum here in reference to this bugbear of obscurity. We do not skip Shakespeare or Dante because we must labor with them. It is conceded that neither Emerson nor Browning can be called pellucid writers. What they bring requires a faculty for resolving, not wholly dissimilar to that which inheres in the contribution. Is it unfair that the reader should be asked to possess a little spark of the fire that went with so much force to inflame the page?

But there is a difference in opacities. Emerson's dimness seems more directly a necessary incident, and less an invention. It is not so willful-appearing as the English poet's. If he exploits new idioms in his speech he is not so full of incessant syntactical contractions—the verb and its nominative case and all the parts of speech scintillating and careering about until their condition becomes as doubtful as was Douglas Jerrold's when, accosting "Sordello," he felt obliged to ask, "Am I drunk, or am I sober?" Nor is there such a conglomeration of broken sentences gluing together fragments of thought which he begins to utter, and then drops, as Browning uses—leaving you to pursue your way out of darkness into light as best you may.

Emerson's opacity relates more logically and reasonably to the magnitude of his thought. Apart from it all, however, he has, as I shall show, abundant fluid beauty, which ought to be familiar and accessible to any reader to whom the best poetry has anything to offer. He uses "thunder-words," as the Germans say, which fill with lightning all the circuits of the sky; but they are there for a purpose. Oftener than anything, I suspect, which troubles the average mind that approaches this incomparably fine body of verse, is its unremitting, tremendous condensation of thought. If Emerson were to touch a trifle, the blow would be delivered with the weight of a trip-hammer; yet, as that instrument is sometimes successfully used to crack a walnut, so his reserve force, always apparent and dominant, gives weight to the most airy expression. He does not certainly write *vers de société*, as Locker and Dobson do; but in his poem of "The Romany Girl" we can see how the lighter theme fares in his hands. It is the gypsy who speaks and says:

> The sun goes down and with him takes
> The coarseness of my poor attire;
> The fair moon mounts, and ay the flame
> Of gypsy beauty blazes higher.
>
> Pale Northern Girls! you scorn our race;
> You captives of your air-tight halls,
> Wear out indoors your sickly days,
> But leave us the horizon walls.
>
> *   *   *   *   *   *
>
> Go, keep your cheek's rose from the rain,
> For teeth and hair with shopmen deal:
> My swarthy tint is in the grain—
> The rocks and forests know it real.
>
> The wild air bloweth in our lungs,
> The keen stars twinkle in our eyes,
> The birds gave us our wily tongues,
> The panther in our dances flies.

How well thought out this imagery is. The lines, hard and tensely drawn, fall upon the air with tingling, metallic force. Emerson cannot abide the frail texture so fashionable in a great deal of modern verse, and insists that a spinal system is preferable to mere perfumery, color, and technical correctness. In another brief poem, titled "The Amulet," which is given without reduction below, see with what firmness and force he imprints the intense and scalding thought of the lover, a little while separated from the object of his love, and (so it ever is) of his agonizing doubt:

Your picture smiles as first it smiled;
  The ring you gave is still the same;
Your letter tells, O changing child!
  No tidings *since* it came.

Give me an amulet
  That keeps intelligence with you,—
Red when you love, and rosier red,
  And when you love not, pale and blue.

Alas! that neither bonds nor vows
  Can certify possession;
Torments me still the fear that love
  Died in its last expression.

A purely academic writer, or a feebler genius would not have ventured to invert the verb in the final couplet, or to change the music and motion so suddenly as it is done in the first line of the second stanza. He would probably have said, in the latter instance:

Give me a *trusty* amulet,

or would have used some other adjective to piece out a uniform rhythm. But this broken chord exactly fits the sudden shock of eagerness and passion at that particular moment. A great musician puts in discords purposely, which the full piece resolves; but your Fadladeens, who know how to "judge of everything, from the pencilling of a Circassian's eyelids to the deepest questions of science and literature," see only the technical deficiency or redundance, as the case may be.

Among the few poems which Emerson
has keyed to the lighter movement, I
have always thought his "Una" stands
conspicuous for an ineffable, haunting
beauty, which, if I could, I should not
care to explain. With what captivating
touches he has shaped these stanzas and
couplets which I take from it below:

> Roving, roving, as it seems,
> Una lights my clouded dreams;
> Still for journeys she is dressed;
> We wander far by east and west.
>
> *   *   *   *   *   *   *
>
> If from home chance draw me wide,
> Half-seen Una sits beside.
>
> *   *   *   *   *   *   *
>
> But if upon the seas I sail,
> Or trundle on the glowing rail,
> I am but a thought of hers,
> Loveliest of travelers.

One can best understand the nature of
Emerson's poetry by taking some account

of the view-point, or perspective, which he employs. His own conception of what it is that goes to the making of the true bard will in some measure define his own position. I open his oldest book of poems almost by accident at " Merlin," and hear him say:

> The trivial harp will never please
> Or fill my craving ear ;
> Its chords should ring as blows the breeze,
> Free, peremptory, clear.
> No jingling serenader's art,
> Nor tinkle of piano-strings,
> Can make the wild blood start
> In its mystic springs.
> The kingly bard
> Must smite the chords rudely and hard,
> As with hammer or with mace ;
> That they may render back
> Artful thunder, which conveys
> Secrets of the solar track,
> Sparks of the supersolar blaze.

> *   *   *   *   *   *   *

> Great is the art,
> Great be the manners, of the bard.

He shall not his brain encumber
With the coil of rhythm and number;   .
But, leaving rule and pale forethought,
He shall ay climb
For his rhyme.
" Pass in, pass in," the angels say,
" In to the upper doors,
Nor count compartments of the floors,
But mount to paradise
By the stair-way of surprise."

*   *   *   *   *   *   *

He shall not seek to weave,
In weak, unhappy times,
Efficacious rhymes ;
Wait his returning strength.
Bird, that from the nadir's floor
To the zenith's top can soar,
The soaring orbit of the muse exceeds that
    journey's length.

I detect an almost playful Persian touch
in the final cadences of this extract, as if
the author were mounting to his purpose
" by the stair-way of surprise "—or, as if
Hafiz or Firdousi himself were speaking.
It is said that Persian poetry—and, in fact,

all oriental verse — admits of endless license
in the matter of rhythm and versification,
there being no less than three systems of
metre, marked by different rules, which need
not be kept separate, and which are often
allowably made to coalesce in a single
piece. But Emerson not only takes an
oriental freedom in his measures; he employs, as the Asiatic bards do, all the
machinery of subtle, unexpected and fantastic conceit. His sensitive harp catches
in the air many tones. You find echoes of
Marlowe, Chapman, Milton, Marvell, Her-
bert, Herrick, and Donne, and of all schools;
chords which go round the world and
through the centuries; and notably that
rich, that prodigal, luxurious, quintessential
attar which flows from the realm of the
rising sun. What Goethe says of the
Spanish poet Calderon (I quote Lord
Houghton's forcible translation) serves

equally well if you substitute for his name Emerson's:

> Many a light the Orient throws,
> O'er the midland waters brought;
> He alone who Hafiz knows
> Knows what Calderon has thought.

In the "May-Day" volume some of Emerson's own characteristic epigram verses (the "Quatrains") are placed in juxtaposition to his terse translations, chiefly oriental, and the kinship of the mintage is, in some respects, curious. Shall we say on account of this homogeneity that the Oriental is but another Yankee? Or is it that the Yankee is merely the Oriental moved farther west. At any rate, what Hafiz addresses to himself, and what Emerson says of him, are wondrously alike in mood, texture, and tune. This is what Hafiz sings:

> Thou foolish Hafiz! say, do churls
> Know the worth of Oman's pearls?
> Give the gem which dims the moon
> To the noblest, or to none.

And this is Emerson's portraiture which follows:

> Her passions the shy violet
> From Hafiz never hides;
> Love-longings of the raptured bird
> The bird to him confides.

Nor is the generic similarity of which I speak, which these two quatrains partially indicate, all owing to the fact that Emerson puts his own flavor into the translation. The truth is, if the translation here seems (as it evidently does) a little more like Emerson than it does like Hafiz, the balance is more than preserved by his steeping his own original quatrain in a little tincture of the wine and spirit of oriental thought. When he translated Hafiz, he was probably thinking of his own workmanship; when he described him, he was simply absorbed in the *milieu* of the Persian poet.

One of his draughts on the Persian muse, which is so alive and fluent that it fairly

sings and dances itself into the reader's
brain, is the mystic "Song of Seid Nimetollah
of Kuhistan," which is sung and danced by
the Dervishes in one of their religious exer-
cises. I give only the first stanza — but the
whole is worth the reader's attention:

> Spin the ball! I reel, I burn,
> Nor head from foot can I discern,
> Nor my heart from love of mine,
> Nor the wine-cup from the wine.
> All my doing, all my leaving,
> Reaches not to my perceiving;
> Lost in whirling spheres I rove,
> And know only that I love.

Saadi's objective verses — the ethics and
anecdote of "The Gulistan" — have also
won the high regard and compliment of
Emerson. Many of his devoted readers
will recall, before they reach this reference
to it, his enthusiastic article on "Persian
Poetry," published twenty years ago in the
Atlantic Monthly, in which he interspersed,

with great relish, bits and nuggets of various authors, drawn from Von Hammer Purgstall's Persian anthology.

It is difficult, I find, to speak of Emerson's poetry without frequently thinking over or stepping over the line which separates it from his prose — the spiritual borderland being so faint, elusive, and indefinite. Both have been often accused of being inconsecutive — " not logical, but analogical," as Alcott says — a disarranged jumble of shining thoughts; and I note, in Emerson's preface to Gladwin's translation of " The Gulistan," that he says: " Wonderful is the inconsecutiveness of the Persian poets. * * * No topic is too remote for their rapid suggestion. The Ghaselle, or Kassida, is a chapter of proverbs, or proverbs unchaptered,— unthreaded beads of all colors, sizes, and values. Out of every ambush these leap on the unwary reader." Of Saadi, he says: "Through his Persian dialect he speaks to all nations, and like Homer, Shakespeare, Cervantes, and Montaigne, is perpetually modern." In his long poem dedicated to this serene old bard—who is said to have divided his life up into sections of about thirty years for experience, meditation, and travel, and who devoted the last thirty and more of them, until he died, aged 102, to meditation and literary work—Emerson says:

> His words, like a storm-wind, can bring
> Terror and beauty on their wing;
> In his every syllable
> Lurketh nature veritable;
> And though he speak in midnight dark,—
> In heaven no star, on earth no spark,—
> Yet before the listener's eye
> Swims the world in ecstasy.
> The forest waves, the morning breaks,
> The pastures sleep, ripple the lakes,
> Leaves twinkle, flowers like persons be,
> And life pulsates in rock or tree.
> Saadi, so far thy words shall reach;
> Suns rise and set in Saadi's speech!

How dearly Emerson likes a deep and wide utterance. He welcomes and hugs the thought which sweeps over a broad swath. Nothing less than the whole curve which reaches from sunrise to sunset will satisfy him. It is our littleness, our monotony — he would tell us — that reprobates a foreign garb of speech, or terms a remote manner provincial. The universality, scope, and depth which he attains give to his outlines the breadth and largeness of cartoons which rest against an unlimited background. The extent of his draught, like that which Thor took from the drinking-horn of the giants at Jötunheim, seems to imply an oceanic ebb and the motion of cosmic currents.

I am perpetually impressed with the high majesty and solemnity of Emerson's muse. If it touches anything trivial or commonplace, it does not leave it so. " When we speak of the poet in any high sense," he writes, " we are driven to such examples as Zoroaster and Plato, St. John and Menu, with their moral burdens." If the spiritual purpose and pretension of the old Greek oracles stood buttressed behind its utterance, it could not well be more earnest or more oracular. How he uses and respects his art may be judged by this extract from his poem of " The Problem."

Not from a vain or shallow thought
His awful Jove young Phidias brought;
Never from lips of cunning fell
The thrilling Delphic oracle;
Out from the heart of nature rolled
The burdens of the Bible old;
The litanies of nations came,
Like the volcano's tongue of flame,
Up from the burning core below,—
The canticles of love and woe;
The hand that rounded Peter's dome
And groined the aisles of Christian Rome,

Wrought in a sad sincerity;
Himself from God he could not free;
He builded better than he knew,—
The conscious stone to beauty grew.

A sense of dignity and reverent beauty transfuses his artistic expression, and is never absent from his thought. The artist, whoever he be—in the Emersonian horoscope—works in "love and terror." He translates the soul of things; and, faithfully spelling out the elusive secrets of Nature and the human heart, finds that he, too, is adjudged a part of the great scheme.

In the same poem he says:

Earth proudly wears the Parthenon,
As the best gem upon her zone;
And morning opes with haste her lids
To gaze upon the Pyramids;
O'er England's abbeys bends the sky,
As on its friends, with kindred eye,—
For, out of thought's interior sphere,
These wonders rose to upper air;

And Nature gladly gave them place,
Adopted them into her race,
And granted them an equal date
With Andes and with Ararat.

Who, now, is the poet that Emerson recognizes, and how shall we describe him? In a suggestive summary he puts the traits of this interpreter in the opening of his exquisite "Woodnotes":

When the pine tosses its cones
To the song of its waterfall tones,
Who speeds to the woodland walks?
To birds and trees who talks?
Cæsar of his leafy Rome,
There the poet is at home.
He goes to the river-side,—
Not hook nor line hath he;
He stands in the meadows wide,—
Nor gun nor scythe to see:
Sure some god his eye enchants:
What he knows nobody wants.

*　　*　　*　　*　　*

Knowledge this man prizes best
Seems fantastic to the rest:

Pondering shadows, colors, clouds,
Grass-buds and caterpillar-shrouds,
Boughs on which the wild bees settle,
Tints that spot the violet's petal,
Why Nature loves the number five,
And why the star-form she repeats :
Lover of all things alive,
Wonderer at all he meets,
Wonderer chiefly at himself,
Who can tell him what he is ?
Or how meet in human elf
Coming and past eternities ?

The poet, then, in this stoutly painted character, is not to be divorced from a certain religious sanctity—an almost priestly habit—a mediatorship between the ineffable and man. And I know of none in the whole range of literature who so answers to this conception as Emerson. This fiber is illustrated by the circumstance that, in lineage, he is the product of eight generations, from no one of which, either on the paternal or maternal side, was the minister absent. The fact of this long ministerial descent enables Burroughs, who has uttered some vivid sayings about his prose, to declare of him that "the blood in his veins has been teaching and preaching, and thinking and growing austere these many generations. * * The virtues of all those New England ministers and all those tomes of sermons are in this casket."

It is a strong spiritual effluence you extract from all he prints, either in prose or verse—a savor of Sinai and the moral law. He plants the flower edelweiss and alpine beauty on these high glaciers. A most importunate and patient searcher he is after the inmost meaning of things. He would miss nothing that is significant; he will crowd the universe into a nutshell, and makes every line bear the burden that weaker writers bestow on a whole page. It is the very pith and marrow of the matter which he wishes to unfold; and nothing satisfies him that is less than a piercing stroke into the deep below the deep.

With what pure selection he chooses every word. His whole life-time has gone into the making of a few volumes — not much more than half a dozen in all — and the longer he lives the more he cramps and bereaves them; but what wit, and strength, and beauty, and eloquence they uphold! What a supreme, audacious splendor! In the slow manner in which he writes, and erases; in the long time he holds his proof-sheets for perusal, reperusal, and retouching of the text, to the great perplexity of his publishers (if they have not long since become used to it),—is shown the intense thoroughness and winnowing he applies to each separate part and piece. In his poem *

* The muse which speaks here is the World-Muse; or, as Mr. Kennedy says, the Genius of Life; but, in a more limited sense, the process described justifies my illustration.

of " The Test" *(Musa Loquitur)* he betrays
with what searching scrutiny each line is
put into final shape:

> I hung my verses in the wind,
> Time and tide their faults may find.
> All were winnowed through and through,
> Five lines lasted sound and true,
> Five were smelted in a pot
> Than the South more fierce and hot—
> These the siroc could not melt;
> Five their fiercer flaming felt,
> And the meaning was more white
> Than July's meridian light.
> Sunshine cannot bleach the snow,
> Nor time unmake what poets know.
> Have you eyes to find the five
> Which five hundred did survive?

Endless and persistent with him is this
fiery expurgation, collation, and revision.
" In reading prose," he says, " I am sensitive as soon as a sentence drags, but in
poetry as soon as one word drags." Such
a value he puts upon perfect expression.
A properly termed extemporaneous utter-

ance is not natural with him, and, when he seems to have yielded to occasional utterance, as in the " Hymn " written for the completion of the Concord monument, and one or two other pieces, the exceptions are voided of force by the probable coincidence of a genuine inspiration with the occasion. But the theory which rules his habit is not left without proof. In one of his earliest essays, he confides to his readers that "the inexorable rule in the muse's court, *either inspiration or silence*, compels the bard to report only his supreme moments. It teaches the enormous force of a few words, and in proportion to the inspiration checks loquacity." As his beloved Herrick says:

'Tis not every day that I
Fitted am to prophesy.
No; but when the spirit fills
The fantastic pinnacles

Full of fire, then I write
As the Godhead doth indite.
Thus enraged my lines are hurled,
Like the Sibyls, through the world.
Look, how next the holy fire
Either slakes, or doth retire;
So the fancy carols, till when
That brave spirit comes again.

It is interesting to compare the poems as they stand in his first book with the book now current, which contains everything already offered in book form that he cares to preserve. The real changes are not so many; but some of the most competent and loyal lovers of Emerson's poetry grieve at any change. They hesitate in having any line that he has ever written blotted or blurred. I discern in the latest volume four poems that I do not find in either of the two volumes preceding it, viz.: " April," " Maiden Speech of the Æolian Harp," " Cupido," and

" The Nun's Aspiration," besides a few
that have been picked out of his magazine contributions of later years. Another,
entitled simply " The Harp," is merely a
long episode taken from " May-Day " as
it first appeared; and this " May-Day "
poem has itself undergone in its new
guise, in addition to this long elision, a
variety of permutations similar to that
which would happen if half its paragraphs
were to be taken and shuffled like a pack
of cards. The traditional critic would sig-
nal this as an evidence of invalidity in
the poem, but the admirer of Emerson
sees in the fact that it survives such a
shock the deep spiritual content of it, and
feels that it has filaments which secure its
unity against all accidents of disrupted
logical succession or mere verbal weld-
ing. Sufficient to each part is its own
meaning, while each also conspires to a

ravishing wholeness quite beyond an ordinary writer's reach. A few lines I find are omitted, but the transformation is the chief change.

In the "Woodnotes," the first six lines are omitted, and those which immediately follow are accommodated to this change; but farther on a large paragraph is discarded, and a considerable part of another is placed in the section marked Part II. In Part II. there are fewer changes; but these electric lines, among others, are missing :

> I will teach the bright parable
> Older than time,
> Things undeclarable,
> Visions sublime.

In "Waldeinsamkeit," the last line of the first stanza is wholly changed, and the penultimate stanza is omitted. In "Merlin," Part II. is entirely omitted from the revised poems. These do not include all the changes; but I do not care to complete the list, or to say more about them than to remark that, when allowance is made for what is wholly left out or simply re-arranged, there were but few verbal or essential modifications that seemed fit to be made even to the author's fastidious judgment.* I notice a typographical error occurs in the new edition at the end of Part I. of the " Woodnotes," which makes the final line end with a comma joined to a dash. My copy of this edition bears date of 1879; though I also possess, and have at hand, the first edition (copyright of 1846) and the " May-Day " collection. These three books contain, with the exception of a part of the motto-poems in " The Conduct of Life " and other prose works, all of Emerson's poetry, I be-

* See Appendix.

lieve, that has so far found its way into
covers.

As a pendant to the bibliographical side
of my subject, I venture to think the following poem, written by Emerson when he
was twenty-six years old, and which has
never appeared in any edition of his works,
will be of interest to the reader. I am indebted for it to a friend whose copy of it
bears a preface by Col. T. W. Higginson,
which says, "it is taken from a little volume
called *The Offering*, which was published by
the Cambridge Divinity Students in 1829."
While its intrinsic value is not small, it
piques curiosity from the fact that it exhibits
the early groping of the author's mind
toward its present mold of form :

FAME.

Ah, Fate! cannot a man
　　Be wise without a beard?
From East to West, from Beersheba to Dan,
　　Say, was it never heard

That wisdom might in youth be gotten,
Or wit be ripe before 'twas rotten?

He pays too high a price
    For knowledge and for fame
Who gives his sinews to be wise,
    His teeth and bones to buy a name,
And crawls through life a paralytic,
To earn the praise of bard and critic.

Is it not better done,
    To dine and sleep through forty years,
Be loved by few, be feared by none,
    Laugh life away, have wine for tears,
And take the mortal leap undaunted,
Content that all we ask was granted?

But Fate will not permit
    The seeds of gods to die,
Nor suffer sense to win from wit
    Its guerdon in the sky;
Nor let us hide, whate'er our pleasure,
The world's light underneath a measure.

Go, then, sad youth, and shine!
    Go, sacrifice to fame;
Put love, joy, health, upon the shrine,
    And life to fan the flame!
Thy hapless self for praises barter,
And die to Fame an honored martyr.

I do not forget the fact that some wise and cultured people are confounded by Emerson's poetry. It is portentous and unfathomable, and they skip the page which offers them nothing. Like some who dislike Wagner's music, they have never yet felt the key-note. A critical English journal has made the unqualified declaration that Emerson is not a poet; and what, for the want of a real academy, we may term academical tradition, sides largely with the dissidents. But argument is as futile with this state of mental inaptitude as it is with the color-blind. There is no delinquency of perception so unhelpable as that which discerns but one literary fashion. A candid and broader view will not believe that beauty exhausts itself in a single type. Genius is for the most part a law unto itself, and is usually the element which is certain to escape your most precise definition. You demand a logical order, and do not find it. Remember, to the careless eye the clear stars of a winter evening are but so many single points; but to the astronomer, the mechanism of the universe, and the music of the spheres of which they are the symbols, are not less imagined and real.

I find in Emerson's poetry (and the observation touches his prose as well) a constant relation to the breadth of some endless horizon. Each line is an arrow swept across, or into the center of the universe; and it is not a common divinity that has drawn the bow. "The poet," he says, "gives us the eminent experience only — a god stepping from peak to peak, nor planting his foot but on a mountain." "Jewels all," says Alcott. "Separate stars," * * but, "vistas opening far and wide." * * "There is substance, sod, sun; much fair weather in the seer as in his

4

leaves. The whole quaternion of the seasons, the sidereal year has been poured into these periods. Afternoon walks furnished their perspective, rounded and melodized them." It is the art of Emerson to load and overload his words with the most urgent stress of beauty and meaning. They are suggestive in unnamable directions, and, as Lowell says, "fecundative"—"a divining-rod to our deeper natures." Channing says of them:

The circles of thy thought shine vast as stars,
    No glass shall round them,
    No plummet sound them,
They hem the observer like bright steel-wrought bars,
    And limpid as the sun,
    Or as bright waters run
From the cold fountain of the Alpine springs,
Or diamonds richly set in the king's rings.

What force and grace stream from lines like these, where he terms the Humble-bee

Thou animated torrid zone!

*   *   *   *   *   *

Sailor of the atmosphere;
Swimmer through the waves of air;
Voyager of light and noon;
Epicurean of June;

and one may read as well for the same qualities the whole poem. Or these lines below, taken with little selection from " May-Day ":

The youth reads omens where he goes,
And speaks all languages the rose.

*   *   *   *   *   *   *

Is it Dædalus? Is it love?
Or walks in mask almighty Jove,
And drops from Power's redundant horn
All seeds of beauty to be born?

*   *   *   *   *   *   *

But soft! a sultry morning breaks;
The ground-pines wash their rusty green,
The maple-tops their crimson tint,
On the soft path each track is seen,
The girl's foot leaves its neater print.
The pebble loosened from the frost
Asks of the urchin to be tost.

Or read the second and final paragraphs in the " Ode to Beauty," or the whole of " The Rhodora," " The Snow-Storm," the " Two Rivers," and " The Sea-Shore." Where did an elegy ever strike more touching depths than the incomparable " Threnody " ? What farewell to the muse, or to authorship, will you find more tender or pathetic than " Terminus " ? But the aggravation of quoting from our author is, that you leave so much which might just as well be quoted. To attempt this exercise is also to incur the grievous disappointment described in his poem " Each and All," where the " sparrow in his nest " and the " delicate sea-shells " were taken from the large setting which gave them their prime significance. I cannot drop my reference to the " Threnody," however, without repeating what a gifted English poet—who is a felicitous critic by inter-

vals—has uttered with reference to elegiac
verse. He says that the "Lycidas" of
Milton, the "Adonaïs" of Shelley, and
" The Thyrsis " of Matthew Arnold, are
" three elegiac poems so great that they
eclipse and efface all the elegiac poetry
we know ; all of Italian, all of Greek."
Noting, as he does not, Tennyson's long
poem of sorrow as a worthy member of
this group, I must also add to them
Emerson's " Threnody," which, though so
different, is no inferior in this shining
company

The stimulus and inspiration which in-
here in Emerson's words are matchless.
Their melody is not only unique, but
supreme :

> —a melody born of melody,
> Which melts the world into a sea.
> Toil could never compass it,
> Art its height could never hit,
> It came never out of wit.

Burroughs's testimony is that Emerson "has written plenty of poems that are as melodious as the hum of a wild bee in the air—chords of wild æolian music. * * Not in the poetry of any of his contemporaries is there such a burden of the mystery of things or such round wind-harp tones, lines so tense and resonant, and blown upon by a breeze from the highest heaven of thought." And he quotes Rossetti, who says : " He is a Druid who wanders among the bards and strikes the harp with even more than bardic stress."

I admit that Emerson has done what Carlyle did—perfected a mold of speech, in his own way, for himself—and that he does not always obey the prescribed poetical canons; defies them, in fact, with unusual license. He pours forth at times broken, irregular verses; deals in abrupt

transitions of thought; employs occasionally astonishing rhymes; and leaves to the
reader some discretion and part in weaving
together the continuity of his ideas. One
may not think that *down* and *dimension*,
success and *Eumenides*, *bear* and *wood-
pecker*, and the like have any more right
to be married in rhyme, than have the
elephant and the kangaroo; but he puts
them together with a strange felicity, and
the archaism becomes a beauty rather than
a blemish. But I am citing extreme cases
here with full intent. In other couplets—
as in these, for instance—

> Give to barrows, trays, and pans,
> Grace and glimmer of romance;

> Is the ancestor of wars
> And the parent of remorse;

> Love shuns the sage, the child it crowns,
> Gives all to them who all renounce—

' he secures such a flavor as haunts and holds you long after their spell has been uttered. The wish which the poet often feels to get out of ruts, and abandon the Della Cruscan tameness of such frequently repeated rhymes as *day* and *May*, *fly* and *sky*, *breeze* and *trees*, *hour* and *flower*, is easily compassed by Emerson through the virility of his vocabulary, and the strange and subtle force he can put in his final words and syllables — the rhyming chords. The new English school of poets, some-times called the preraphaelites, — of which Swinburne, Rossetti, and Morris are the chiefs, — attain a similar end by making use, with marked effect, of such rhymes as *thing* and *thanksgiving*, *her* and *harp-player*, where the ictus must of necessity fall, in the rhyming word, on the penultimate syllable, instead of on the rhyming one.

It should not be hard for a trained and cultivated ear to acquire a liking for the

magic of Emerson's melody; and when the
mind is in sympathy with the scale of
thought, and beats in time with it, there
befalls a ravishment which unfits the recipi-
ent for any lesser strain. He will no longer
tolerate a thinner tune; the weaker and
watered phrases which before delighted
seem emptied forever of their old charm
and power. It is a music in which color,
aroma, and prismatic light are blended.
Not Offenbach's—passional, laughter-like
and giddy—but rather a symphony like
Beethoven's, which would pierce, or leave
the gates of paradise ajar. Inevitably there
will be no popular, applauding crowd to
listen. It is keyed for a select group in a
vast cathedral, whose roof is the overarching
sky, and whose long, resounding corridors
are made to awaken the deepest imaginings
of the human soul.

We shall never have a second Emerson,
any more than we shall have a second

Shakespeare. Let us not be afraid to cele-
brate him. We are told that he has limitations—that he could not produce an epic
or a drama, and, most likely, would find it
difficult to write an acceptable love-story
for the magazines and newspapers. He
commits the unpardonable sin, with ortho-
dox theories of literature, in writing about
Shakespeare as he does, and—counter to
all traditions—calling his dramatic power
"secondary." I know that Shakespeare
picked up his plots from Boccaccio and
others; how am I to know that even *he*
had the power to produce a plot? It was
his habit, certainly, to take the most of them
at second hand. But Emerson's argument,
I take it, is that, after they *are* produced,
they are merely the frame for his large
idealism—his masterly, colossal, overpowering, spermatic thought. Can Shakespeare
get, did any one ever get, one stroke

beyond the power of pure, primitive thought? Does any one hold that there is a *primum mobile* in mere mechanism? Finally, is not all this talk about the splendor of the drama, because it is drama —the glory of the epos or tale—simply so much laudation of the spoon from which we eat and drink? Or can the vehicle supersede and sanctify the thing that is conveyed?

I am as much captivated by the delicious charm of stories and dramatic situations as any one can be. Childhood not only craves this pleasure, but we ourselves never outgrow the child-like desire to behold a social orrery in which persons take the places of planets, and range through their related orbits. If a few minds—notably Emerson's —have outgrown the necessity for these crutches to help them walk, these glasses to help them see, and can dispense with

literary jack-straws, or complicated lay-
figures, must they be set down as fatally
bereaved? It is no disparagement to the
drama if we insist that it shall not be pro-
nounced as a shibboleth. Let a master use
what medium he pleases—he shall be a
master still; and whether Emerson is really
limited or self-limited, I hail him as a member of that inspired choir which he describes—one of those

> Olympian bards who sung
> Divine ideas below,
> Which always find us young,
> And always keep us so.

Our delight in Emerson, in fact, springs
largely from his loftiness of vision. His
perspective is that of the aëronaut's, and
he never falls or falters below it. There is
not a line which descends from the first
high level. Such uniformity of altitude no
writer that I know of so steadily maintains.

Here is so high a voice that it never leaves the sunshine — is never swathed in shadows — but, like the final one in Longfellow's " Excelsior," falls

— " like a falling star."

A proverb-like fullness, purity of tone, magnetic phrases, the beating of the Puritan pulse, are in his speech. In his poems, the titles are half-poems. His sentences tingle with tense, metallic vibration. He is a perpetual surprise. You read deep secrets through him as Coleridge read Shakespeare through Kean's acting — "by flashes of lightning." We miss in his page the first note of tumult or turbulence. Two symbols which occur in his prose and recur in his poetry — the Æolian Harp and the Pine-Tree (which is but another Æolian Harp) — fitly express his genius. It is through these that we have access to and communication with the deep, vague whispers of immensity and eternity.

Many years ago Mr. Emerson handed me a slip of paper, at the end of an interview, on which he had written a couplet of his own, which, I think, has never yet found its way into print. I give it below because it partakes of his essential quality, and also because it helps me to point a reflection. Thus it reads:

> A score of airy miles will smooth
> Rough Monadnock to a gem.

The alert reader will perceive at once that this thought is substantially equivalent in purport to Campbell's well-worn distich below:

> 'Tis distance lends enchantment to the view,
> And robes the mountains in their azure hue.

But one is delicate, suggestive; the other direct and prosaic. The first is cloth of silk and gold; the second is calico, in comparison, or, perhaps, fustian. He who makes choice between these two forms discloses and defines his own measure of poetic perception—puts himself on the empyreal summit, or settles in the shallows of commonplace.

It cannot be too often repeated that Emerson's poetry is, above all its felicities, alive with moral purport and motive. Emerson no more deals in art for art's sake than you build your house for the display of a cornice and picturesque angles. What he has to say leaps forth from an overpowering burden—a weight of compulsion restrained up to the point of the irresistible. His poetry is not so much made as it is received and retold. It is the mouth-piece of the moral sentiment, the transpiration of original and primitive promptings—the breath of the Oversoul.

And yet there is no part of its form that is not carefully studied and shaped. The most wayward line, the most frolicsome paragraph, as the indentations and type run, are adjusted after a strictly studied and conscientious plan. The pedant, whose sense of scansion and balanced rhythm never went farther than Pope's heroic couplet, looks up confounded at it, and thinks he has discovered an escape from Bedlam. He finds his "settled literary opinions and tastes disturbed," and he has no conception of any other.

The late Prof. Reed, who made some acute observations on this limited literary sense, said: "It is the highest attribute of original powers to enlarge the sphere of human sensibility. Think, for instance, how the light of Spenser's imagination at once disclosed to view the untraveled latitudes of his mavelous allegory. * * * When a poet of original powers arises, his very originality can be shown only by extending the light of his genius to regions of thought and feeling unillumined before." In another place he says: "Each poet of original genius dwells in an atmosphere of his own, and he who seeks to know him must learn to breathe it. * * He must needs live in it for a brief space."

Emerson's attitude to the universe has a certain resemblance to Swedenborg's, but is without the slightest touch, though, of that hallucinated seer's dogma, and coarse, mechanical contrivance. He reports from an immanent spirit the closest correspondences between the soul and material expression. There is no limit to his reverent wonder; even the slightest thing takes on the hue of miracle. I am often reminded, by his manner of evolving his verses, of Wordsworth's curious child,

— applying to his ear
The convolutions of a smooth-lipped shell.

5

As the roaring sea, unseen and afar off, spoke to his inland imagination, evoking continual awe and wonder, so the earth, sky, and sea speak to Emerson. His rapture with Nature rises to perennial inspiration—to a serene, excessive delight. Shown equally in a score of examples, I only quote here, as an instance, the conclusion to " The Rhodora ":

Rhodora ! if the sages ask thee why
This charm is wasted on the earth and sky,
Tell them, dear, that if eyes were made for seeing,
Then beauty is its own excuse for being:
Why thou wert there, O rival of the Rose!
I never thought to ask—I never knew;
But, in my simple ignorance, suppose
The self-same power that brought me there
    brought you.

This ecstasy and raptness melt at times into a subtle mysticism, or burst into Hebraic austerity of enunciation. In moods like these the oracular voice becomes, occasionally, so intent on its utterance, as to appear enigmatic and puzzling. Perhaps the quatrain given below, written for Mrs. Sargent, and which Emerson himself has never printed, will exhibit what I suggest. It is a miniature sermon on charity; and I am quoting Mr. Sanborn, I think, in saying that we have here "his exact oracular words, such as he chooses for verse, leaving the reader to make the best of them, and careless if he sometimes makes the worst of them "·

> The beggar begs by God's command,
> And gifts awake when givers sleep:
> Swords cannot cut the giving hand,
> Nor stab the love that orphans keep.

It is Mr. Sanborn, at any rate, who says this apropos of Emerson's verse: "It is the privilege of exquisite beauty, and of that nobility of soul which is the counterpart and masculine response to beauty, instantly to deprive us of all power of comparison. They are like nothing in our experience, they suggest nothing but themselves and each other, and in their brightness all things else appear but as dust in the sunshine. Whoever has not had this vision, nor felt this kindling of the soul in reading or listening to Emerson, must have failed to meet his thought at all, and therefore be as incapable of understanding him as the deaf are to appreciate music. * * It was said of Socrates, in a doubtful compliment, that he brought philosophy down from heaven to earth. It might as truly be said of Emerson that he raises earth to the level of divine philosophy—a loftier art. His method in this is a purely poetic one, and therefore, while he lacks what is ordinarily called creative power in verse, he moves more constantly than any recent poet in the atmosphere of poesy. Since Milton and Spenser, no man—not even Goethe—has equaled Emerson in this trait, which, like personal beauty, as has been said, can neither be explained nor criticised. 'There it is. If you do not see it, God help you! for none of us can!'"

A brilliant French writer remarks that well-selected words are sentences abridged. Schelling says, "In good prose every word is underscored." It was a favorite saying of the Pandits that "an author rejoiceth in the economizing of half a short vowel as much as in the birth of a son!" Apter illustrations of this emphasis of brevity cannot be found than in Emerson's style. How constantly he surprises by not only pressing all the meaning out of a word, but by crowding voluminous and unsuspected force into it? All his

verses bristle with this power. Mr. F. H.
Hedge pronounces his poem of "The
Problem" as "wholly unique, and tran-
scending all contemporary verse in grandeur
of style." Of all the poems Frederika
Bremer said: "They are all to me as a
breeze from the life of the New World, in a
certain illimitable vastness of life, in expec-
tation, in demand, in faith, in hope,—a
something which makes me draw a deeper
breath, and, as it were, in a larger and freer
world." Joined to this strength is the web
and spell of beauty from which he never for
a moment escapes. What he says of Saadi,
in a part of a fragment of one poem not yet
submitted by him to the public, fits equally
his own gift:

> Northward he went to the snowy hills;
> At court he sat in grave Divan.
> His music was the south-wind's sigh,
> His lamp the maiden's downcast eye;
> And ever the spell of Beauty came,

And turned the drowsy world to flame,
By lake, and stream, and gleaming hall,
And modest copse and forest tall,
Where'er he went, the magic guide
Kept its place by the poet's side.

If we return now to the previous question, and ask, What is poetry? a thousand answers confront us. When Joubert said that " Boileau is a powerful poet, but only in the world of half poetry," his final phrase flashed with illumination. " How true that is of Pope also!" says Matthew Arnold. To many, poetry is indissolubly confounded with a counting of their fingers; and a consciousness of this prevalent faith made an irreverent critic say that any one who can measure tape can write the poetry of Pope. The witty *mot* had a grain of truth under its extravagance, but overlooked Pope's prodigal power in one direction. No sane critic now, I am sure, considers the " Essay on Man" as anything more than an admirable piece of worldly wit put in rhymed epigram. Still, it is the best " half poetry " that the world of the eighteenth century had to show. Poetry that is whole, or entire, has for its fountain-head the imagination; but this is a theme too large for subsidiary discussion, or for treatment as an episode.

Carlyle's averment that poetry is " musical thought " is good enough so far as it goes. And, if we take what he himself says of music, the description applies perfectly to some of the deep and far-away tones of Emerson's muse. That haunting, undulating thrill which captivates the soul and defies expression pulses through, and is in, the very midst of it. Its offering cannot always be translated into exact phrases—meaning so much and no more; for it is " a kind of inarticulate, unfathomable speech, which leads us to the edge of the Infinite, and lets us for moments gaze into that!"

Emerson's genius—though it contains, as I have said, the core and heart of the East—is, in form, essentially Northern and Gothic; not tropical, or equatorial. It has a hyperborean birth, and sometimes shows a touch of sturdy Berserker wrath. The volcano within is capped with ice and snow above—emotion subservient to intellect. It is power, passion, infinite restraint, and repose working in unison. The beauty of his lines has sometimes the effect upon me of an arctic landscape. I walk through the enchantments of Niflheim. I see the splendors of icebergs and ice-clad forests, frosty stalactites and prismatic wonders, gleaming auroras, and all that gives a crystalline delight. And yet, if you interpret the fable so as to make it mean the *spiritually* dead, it is "poetry which, like the verses inscribed on Balder's column at Breidablik, is capable of restoring the dead to life." Its regenerative power cannot be measured to those who have once caught the focus of the lens. If you look toward it from the dull end of the kaleidoscope, you will see only a handful of colored beads. Put your eye on the right line, and you cannot shuffle them or jostle them from the most serene and exquisite purpose and order.

I do not expect the world will be converted to the enthusiasm that requires so much preparation to receive, or that there will ever be a popular deference to, Emerson's mode and perspective. I know how much easier it is to toy with and enjoy the colored surfaces of things than to explore the higher altitudes, or penetrate into the abysmal depths. "Men," says Bacon, "prefer to the diamond the deeper-colored gems." The telling objects to the majority are the transparent ones, and the average reader, only aroused languidly, cares for nothing but that note which

"Rings like a tinkling pebble down a tinkling path."

Whoever chooses to reflect sees there is an essence of poetry which none of the definitions perfectly define. That dainty genius, Joubert, who writes as if Ariel had turned critic, says: " The poet must be not only the Phidias and the Dædalus of his verses; he must also be the Prometheus: with form and movement he must also give them life." Accosting the perplexing problem that has come down to us from the time of Aristotle, he puts himself among the questioners on this theme. Asking " What is poetry? " he replies: " At this moment I cannot say. But I maintain that, in words used by the true poet, there is found for the eyes a certain phosphorous, for the taste a certain nectar, for the attention an ambrosia not found in them when used by any one else." Was there ever any one to whom this description applies better than it does to Emerson?

Is there any one now living — is there any old Greek master among the dead — who ever spoke with more majestic or sonorous, more strident, more enchanting or more appealing emphasis, than the one we have dared to extol? Where shall we find the fountain of beauty, if his words are not bathed in it? Where the sea of thought, or the sky of imagination, if his pinions have not touched them?

One profound New England scholar, widely versed in various literatures, and himself a poet, has very lately said: " I place Emerson at the head of the lyric poets of America. In this judgment I anticipate wide dissent." But he explains, after going so far, that he does not so much refer to his poetic art, in which he recognizes limitations, as to his "utter spontaneity. * * More than any one of his contemporaries, his poems for the most part are inspirations. They are not made, but given; they come of themselves." He speaks of them as "bursting from the soul with an irrepressible necessity of utterance — sometimes with a rush that defies the shaping intellect." It has been noted by more than one that he has written lines that are now as well established as those we quote from Shakespeare. Take, as a ready instance:

He builded better than he knew;

or that line from another poem:

And fired the shot heard round the world;
or,
"The silent organ loudest chants
The master's requiem."

Nature, tremulous with mind, and not
a soulless mechanism, is the great affirma-
tion which runs not only through Emerson's poetry, but through all that he writes.
To illustrate this, he commands every re-
source and makes even the denials of
science fortify the truth on which the universe is suspended. It used to be said
of Wendell Phillips's speeches that they
always give you the latest news; the
evening lecture would be as fresh as the
evening paper; and, after a similar sort,
you can discern the high-water mark—
the lapse of the last wave—of science in
Emerson's periods. Mr. W. T. Harris
says that, "no other poet since Shakespeare has been endowed with so clear
and sustained insight into the transcend-
ency of mind in the visible world."

Of his employment of other factors than
rhythm and rhyme in the formation of his

poems, the same writer gives a felicitous hint. " Emerson," he says, " very often uses the Hebrew device of rhyme of thought in his poetry, though not omitting—if sometimes slighting—the external rhyme and rhythm." And this is illustrated in the following passage from his poem of " The Sphinx ":

> The fate of the man-child;
>   The meaning of man;
> Known fruit of the unknown;
>   Dædalian plan;
> Out of sleeping a waking,
>   Out of waking a sleep;
> Life death overtaking;
>   Deep underneath deep.

To the criticism of poetry Emerson brings a deep insight—an interior vision. It is the spirit, not the mold, which first arrests him. To a genuine inspiration he can allow great latitude of manner and form. In detecting faults, or marking

verbal felicities,—while looking mainly beyond these,—none is better than he. His
emphasis on affirmatives sometimes made
him benignant where others would be
severe; but what he saw was certainly
there. His opinion of poetry, it is said,
had, with his most noted friends, famous
themselves as poets, a high judicial value.
If the world did not heed his work, *they*, at
least, listened to his large and minute
criticism as they listened to no other.
Whatever the press might declare, or public
silence and neglect imply, no great poet
doubts that he stands monumentally high
in his guild.

If there is a seeming exception to this
statement in one young English poet's out-
break when piqued and offended at a little
plain speaking by Emerson over his froth-
fully frenetic and sensual fancies, it finds a
reason in that fact. And yet I do not

doubt that this writer of marvelous gifts in the lyric direction sees and esteems—as his bitter retort does not exclude, and would imply—Emerson's authority and power. In this coupling with Emerson's a name representing such contrast in style, one who thinks of them both can see how Olympian calmness and restraint compare with their extreme counterpart in the field of poetical expression. No doubt Emerson's "Parnassus" revealed in him, to some minds, unexpected tastes and predilections, but it justifies, on careful study, catholicity of feeling and keen discernment.

Mr. Curtis says that Emerson's words, long ago applied to Channing's poetry in *The Dial*, could be easily transformed to describe his own. " It is of such extreme beauty that we do not remember anything more perfect of its kind." Enough casual and confirmative utterances of similar pur-

6

port could be picked up to excuse the lonesomeness of my plea, if it were worth while, or if I cared to occupy much further space on this subject. Mr. Stedman and Mr. Whipple, I believe, are each contemplating considerable essays on Emerson's poetry; while Mr. G. W. Cooke, who has nearly ready* a "A Study of Emerson," will devote a chapter, at least, to its significance and high quality. In a few years, let us hope— for, I take it, these are to be favorable voices—the neglect which has hitherto been conspicuous will begin to be repaired.

It has been remarked that certain pregnant lines from Emerson's poem of " The Problem " have been embalmed in Westminster Abbey; and those who have read

* This book has now appeared under the title, " Ralph Waldo Emerson: His Life, Writings, and Philosophy," and is one of the best tributes that has ever been paid to Emerson's genius and memory.

the one and seen the other cannot well question the felicity of the combination. But we may be permitted to wonder which is bolder, the architecture of the poet, or that of the cathedral.

I am impressed with the necessity, in speaking of Emerson's poetry, of being in a measure paradoxical. If I say the flowing forms of Gothic architecture — that flower of Nature — which you find in this famous abbey symbolize this form of verse, I am compelled also to note in innumerable places its kinship to Doric severity — that flower of Art. Who is it that finds an absence of art (an absence of anything, in fact, but commonplace, which is notably absent) in such lines as these ?

> O tenderly the haughty day
> Fills his blue urn with fire;
> One morn is in the mighty heaven,
> And one in our desire.
>
> —*Fourth of July Ode.*

Guest of million painted forms,
Which in turn thy glory warms!
The frailest leaf, the mossy bark,
The acorn's cup, the rain-drop's arc,
The swinging spider's silver line,
The ruby of the drop of wine,
The shining pebble of the pond,
Thou inscribest with a bond
In thy momentary play,
Would bankrupt Nature to repay.
        —*Ode to Beauty.*

O ostrich-like forgetfulness!
O loss of larger in the less!
Was there no star that could be sent,
No watcher in the firmament,
No angel from the countless host
That loiters round the crystal coast,
Could stoop to heal that only child,
Nature's sweet marvel undefiled,
And keep the blossom of the earth,
Which all her harvests were not worth?
        —*Threnody.*

Need we ask for more transparency than
these lines afford? And is it not our
fault instead of the writer's if they are not
understood? Those who wish for a mere

poetical veneer, or for poetry that goes on with fatal facility, need not, and will not, turn to Emerson.

I have not sought, however, to hide the fact that he has written a great deal which is dark on the first, and, perhaps, on the third, reading. Of his obscurer verses, it must be observed that the theme is habitually the highest. He strikes out one broad synthesis after another in close succession with bewildering prodigality. They are hints rather than finished statements. The words chosen startle by their deep suggestion. Their polarized vitality, rich symbolism, and strong percussion shock the mind, and celestial vistas, or unfathomed deeps, are opened. Who has ever found a passage in all he has written which does not repay, by its pith, *verve*, and soaring impulse, the study it provokes? In the poem of " Brahma " even, which became a

butt of ridicule when it first appeared, the
author expressed some very definite, if
subtle, ideas; so that the critics who laughed
must have seen, at a later day, that they
had merely advertised their ignorance of
the deeply poetical and significant struct-
ure of the Hindu mythology.

The subtlety of his thought in these
graver instances has, too, its analogue in the
awfulness of life itself, which he describes
in a few mystical and wonderfully melodious lines in the older form of " Merlin ":

"Subtle rhymes with ruin rife,
Murmur in the house of life,
Sung by the Sisters as they spin;
In perfect time and measure they
Build and unbuild our echoing clay,
As the two twilights of the day
Fold us music-drunken in."

But, to linger further with my theme,
would lead me too far. The whole matter will be best concluded by borrowing

Lowell's description of a dozen or more years ago, which sets forth his repeated experience in one of Emerson's lecture audiences at Cambridge.

Those who have heard Emerson's lectures know that the original verses sometimes distributed through them—mingled with the melody of the prose — lent them not a little of their highest charm; so that what is true of the one will not seem unfit to depict the other. Lowell says: " I can never help applying to Emerson what Ben Johnson said of Bacon: ' There happened in my time one noble speaker, who was full of gravity in his speaking. His language was nobly censorious. No man ever spake more neatly, more pressly, more weightily, or suffered less emptiness, less idleness in what he uttered. No member of his speech but consisted of his own graces. His hearers could not cough, or look aside from him, without loss. He commanded where he spoke? Those who heard him while their natures were yet plastic, and their mental nerves trembled under the slightest breath of diviner air, will never cease to feel and say :

> "'Was never eye did see that face,
>   Was never ear did hear that tongue,
> Was never mind did mind his grace,
>   That ever thought the travail long;
> But eyes and ears and every thought
> Were with his sweet perfections caught.'"

APPENDIX.

THE late Mr. John A. Dorgan, a young writer of rare promise, and the author of a book of poems, called "Studies," wrote a very able essay, as I remember it now, some eighteen years or more ago, for the *Boston Commonwealth*, on Emerson's poetry, with special reference to the changes made in it. I have not been able to find this, or to recall any part of it for consultation. But, if a vivid impression may be trusted, I am sure it is worth reprinting.

On comparing the early edition of Emerson's poems with the so-called blue-and-gold one of 1865, which I have done, line for line, I find the most numerous changes occur in the poems titled "Astræa" and "Monadnock." A bad typographical error deserves pointing out in this blue-and-gold edition — the substitution of the word *Like* for *Life*, in the seventh line of the second stanza, in the poem of "The Sphinx."

But my reference here would be inexcusably incomplete if I should forget to mention, as a document of interest in this connection, Mr. William Sloane Kennedy's fine article on "The Discarded Poems of Emerson." It appeared in the *Literary World* of Oct. 7, 1882.

AN

EMERSON CONCORDANCE.

Contributed by WILLIAM SLOANE KENNEDY *to the "Literary World," and used here by special permission.*

A PARTIAL INDEX TO

FAMILIAR PASSAGES IN HIS POEMS.

Page-references are to *Selected Poems* [Copyright, 1876, Houghton, Mifflin & Co.]; for the convenience of those using earlier editions, the name of the poem is given with each reference. In making the index, the plan has been to select from each line or paragraph the most striking and significant word or words. Quite a number of poems that appeared in the familiar brown-cloth editions were omitted by Mr. Emerson in the final 1876 edition. He has also changed many lines in the poems given in that edition. Our love for him is so great that we hardly dare say, against his wishes, that we hope every scrap of his poetry will be included in some complete edition, after the expiration of the present copyright. But, certainly, many of the poems he omitted are too good to be lost.

ACADEME. One in the A.—*S. of Nat.*, p. 161.

ACORN'S. The a. cup.—*Ode to Beauty*, p. 81.

ADORNING. Itself with thoughts of thee a.— *Ode to Beauty*, p. 83.

ATOM. No a. worn.—*S. of Nat.*, p. 162.

Here was this a. in full breath
Hurling defiance at vast death.—*Titmouse*,
p. 63.

ATOMS. A. march in June.—*Monadnock*, p. 149.

The journeying a.—*Sphinx*, p. 8.

AUBURN-DELL. Dream the dream of A.-d.—
May-Day, p. 47.

AVOID. When each the other shall a.—*I. D. and C. Love*, p. 110.

AVON. One by A. stream.—*S. of Nat.*, p. 161.

AXIS. He is the a. of the star.—*Woodnotes*, II., p. 140.

AZALEAS. A. flush the island floors.—*May-Day*, p. 48.

BALL. Over the lifeless b.—*Wealth*, p. 170.

The shadow sits close to the flying b.—
Woodnotes, II., p. 138.

BANKRUPT. Would b. nature to repay.—
Ode to Beauty, p. 81.

BARD. The kingly b.—*Merlin*, p. 114.

BE. I rush to B.—*Nun's Aspiration*, p. 185.

BEAD. String Monadnock like a b.—*Monadnock*, p. 150.

BEAUTY. B. 's not beautiful to me.—*Hermione*, p. 94.

    To die for b.—*Beauty*, p. 178.

    Carves the bow of b. there.—*Woodnotes*, II., p. 135.

    B. is its own excuse for being.—*The Rhodora*, p. 58.

BEE. As the b. through the garden ranges.—*Woodnotes*, II., p. 139.

BEFALL. Who shall tell what did b.— *Wealth*, p. 170.

BEFALLS. B. again what once befell. —*May-Day*, p. 47.

BEING. Firm ensign of the fatal b.—*Monadnock*, p. 153.

    Winds of remembering
    Of the ancient b. blow.— *Bacchus*, p. 118.

BELLY. Wine in b. of the grape.—*Bacchus*, p. 117.

BERYL. B. beam of the broken wave.— *Beauty*, p. 198.

BEST. The fiend that man harries
Is love of the b.— *Sphinx*, p. 9.

BIDES. Who b. at home.—*Fate*, p. 89.

BIND. B. the strength of Nature wild.—
Wealth, p. 171.

BIRD. B. trims her to the gale.— *Terminus*,
p. 187.

BIRDS. The punctual b.—*Musketaq.*, p. 166.
O b. your perfect virtues bring.—*May-
Day*, p. 53.
Named without a gun.— *Forbearance*,
p. 77.

BLOOD. Wild b. start.— *Merlin*, p. 114.
Drop of manly b.—*Friendship*, p. 177.
B. of the world.—*Bacchus*, p. 117.

BLUEBIRD. *Musketaq.*, p. 164.
My b.'s note.— *May-Day*, p. 47.

BOAT. This round sky-cleaving b.— *Monadnock*, p. 150.

BOND. Thou inscribest with a b. — *Ode to
Beauty*, p. 81.

BOWERS. What recks such Traveler if the b.
— *Woodnotes*, II., p. 140.

BOY. B. with his games undaunted.— *World-
Soul*, p. 24.

BRAWLERS. Heed not what the b. say.— *Saadi*, p. 37.

BREAD. Than live for b.— *Beauty*, p. 178.

BREEZE. As blows the b.— *Merlin*, p. 114.

BRIDGE. The ruined b.— *Conc. Fight*, p. 202. B. that arched the flood.— *Conc. Fight*, p. 202.

BUILDED. He b. better than he knew.— *The Problem*, p. 14.

BULLET. B. of the earth.— *Monadnock*, p. 152.

BURDENS. B. of the Bible old.— *The Problem*, p. 14.

BUTLER. Drug the cup, thou b. sweet.— *May-Day*, p. 48.

CALENDAR. Into c. months and days.— *Uriel*, p. 19.

CANISTER. God fills the scrip and c.— *Woodnotes*, II., p. 130.

CANTICLES. The c. of love and woe.— *Problem*, p. 14.

CAPTAIN. Who is the c. he knows not.— *Monadnock*, p. 152.

CARNIVAL. Gods kept c.—*S. of Nat.*, p. 160.

CASCADES. My leaves and my c.—*S. of Nat.*, p. 161.

CENTURIES. Thou meetest him by c.—*Wood-notes*, II., p. 140.

  Gathering along the c.—*S. of Nat.*, p. 159.

CHARMED. Every wave is c.—*Terminus*, p. 187.

CHASTE-GLOWING. C.-g. underneath their lids.—*To Eva*, p. 92.

CHIPS. Who builds yet makes no c.—*Monadnock*, p. 149.

CHOIR. Mighty c. descends.—*I. D. and C. Love*, p. 104.

CHURCH. I like a c.—*The Problem*, p. 16.

CHURCHMAN. That cowled c. be.—*The Problem*, p. 14.

CIPHER. We cannot read the c.—*World-Soul*, p. 25.

CIRCLES. The c. of that sea are laws.—*I. D. and C. Love*, p. 109.

CITIES. What if Trade sow c.—*World-Soul*, p. 26.

7

CLERK. The spruce c.—*Monadnock*, p. 151.

CLIMB. Aye c. for his rhyme.—*Merlin*, p. 115.

CLUB-MOSS. Running over the c.-m. burrs.—*Each and All*, p. 13.

COCKLES. Like c. by the main.—*May-Day*, p. 47.

COINED. Or ever the wild time c.—*Uriel*, p. 18.

COLUMBINE. In c. and clover-blow. — *May-Day*, p. 47.
C. with horn of honey.—*Humblebee*, p. 60.

COMPASS. Toil could never c. it.—*Fate*, p. 88.

CONQUEROR. Alike the c. silent sleeps.—*Conc. Fight*, p. 202.

CONSPIRACY. Works in close c.—*Ode to Beauty*, p. 82.

COOPED. C. in a ship he cannot steer.—*Monadnock*, p. 152.

CORAL. Building in the c. sea.—*S. of Nat.*, p. 160.

CORSE. The glowing angel, the outcast c.—*Woodnotes*, II., p. 140.

COSSACKS. Right C. in their forages. —*I. D. and C. Love*, p. 98.

COURIERS. C. come by squadrons.—*S. of Nat.*, p. 161.

COWARD. Amid these c. shapes.—*Monadnock*, p. 153.

COWL. I like a church; I like a c.—*The Problem*, p. 14.

COWLED. C. portrait dear.—*The Problem*, p. 16.

CRAMP. C. elf and saurian forms.—*S. of Nat.*, p. 160.

CREATION. Ever fresh the broad c.—*Woodnotes*, II., p. 138.

CUP. Brims my little c.—*Day's Ration*, p. 167.

DÆDALIAN. D. plan.—*Sphinx*, p. 7.

DÆMON. Flickering D. film.—*I. D. and C. Love*, p. 108.

The patient D. sits.—*World-Soul*, p. 27.

DAIMON-SPHERE. The path to the d.-s.—*I. D. and C. Love*, p. 103.

DAIMONS. The potent plain of d. spreads.—*I. D. and C. Love*, p. 103.

DAUGHTERS. D. of Time.—*Days*, p. 172.

DAY. Made one of d.—*S. of Nat.*, p. 161.

DAYS. The hypocritic d.—*Days*, p. 172.

DEAD. Happier to be d.—*Beauty*, p. 178.

DEEP. D., d. are loving eyes.—*I. D. and C. Love*, p. 107.

DELICATE. Ever by d. powers.—*S. of Nat.*, p. 159.

DELUGE. Pour the d. still.—*S. of Nat.*, p. 159.

DENS. D. of passion.—*Beauty*, p. 178.

DERVISHES. Like barefoot d.—*Days*, p. 172.

DESPAIR. To master my d.—*Friendship*, p. 177.

DEW. Gives back the bending heavens in d. —*S. of Nat.*, p. 162.

DOFFING. Too much of donning and d.— *S. of Nat.*, p. 161.

DOME. Rounded Peter's d.—*Problem*, p. 14.

DOUBT. Souls above d.—*Give All to Love*, p. 84.

DOUBTER. I am the d. and the doubt.— *Brahma*, p. 73.

DREAD. D. power but dear.— *Ode to Beauty*, p. 83.

DROP. With one d. sheds form and feature.— *Woodnotes*, II., p. 139.

DRUGGED. D. my boy's cup.— *The Sphinx*, p. 9.

DUMB. D. in the pealing song.—*S. of Nat.*, p. 159.

DUTY. D. whispers low, *Thou must.—Voluntaries*, p. 211.

EAGLES. Carries the e.—*Fate*, p. 89.
EARTH-SONG. When I heard the E.-s. *Hamatreya*, p. 72.

ELECTRIC. E. thrills and ties of law.— *Wealth*, p. 171.

ENORMOUS. Through Heaven's e. year.— *Wealth*, p. 170.

ENSIGN. Firm e. of the fatal being.— *Monadnock*, p. 153.

EROS. Strong E. struggling through.— *Beauty*, p. 178.

ESSENCE. He is the e. that inquires.—*Wood-notes*, II., p. 140.

  Holy e. rolls.—*I. D. and C. Love*, p. 108.

ETERNITY. Stars of e. — *Wood-notes*, II., p. 139.

  Ask on thou clothed e.—*The Sphinx*, p. 11.

EVE. Obey the voice at e.— *Terminus*, p. 187.

EYELESS. Plunges e. on forever.— *Monadnock*, p. 152.

FAITHFUL. Lowly f., banish fear.— *Terminus*, p. 187.

FANCY-FREE. Free be she, f.-f.— *Give All to Love*, p. 85.

FANNED. F. the dreams it never brought.— *Woodnotes*, II., p. 130.

FARM - FURROWED. F. - f., town-incrusted sphere.— *Monadnock*, p. 152.

FARMERS. Embattled f.— *Conc. Fight*, p. 202.

FATE. This is he men miscall F.—*Worship*, p. 183.

FATHERS. Our f. built to God.—*Hymn*, p. 200.

FELL. It f. in the ancient periods. *Uriel*, p. 19.

FILLET. Under her solemn f.—*Days*, p. 172.

FIRES. Fanning secret f.—*May-Day*, p. 47.

FISHERS. F. and choppers and ploughmen. —*Bost. Hymn*, p. 204.

FIVE. Why Nature loves the number f.— *Woodnotes*, p. 126.

FLINGS. Into the fifth drop himself he f.— *Woodnotes*, II., p. 139.

FOAM-BELLS. F.-b. along Thought's causing stream.—*World-Soul*, p. 26.

FORGET. F. me if he can.—*Monadnock*, p. 152.

FORM. Gliding through the sea of f.—*Ode to Beauty*, p. 82.

In one only f. dissolves.—*I. D. and C. Love*, p. 108.

FORTHRIGHT. F. my planets roll.—*S. of Nat.*, p. 160.

FOUNT. By the shining f. of life.—*S. of Nat.*, p. 159.

FOUNTAINS. Thou asketh in f. and in fires. —*Woodnotes*, II., p. 140.

F. of my hidden life.—*Friendship*, p. 177.

Spouting f. cool the air.—*Art*, p. 181.

FREEDOM. Ere f. out of man.— *Ode*, p. 208.

FUND. Sober on a f. of joy.— *Waldeinsam-keit*, p. 157.

GALAXY. In globe and g.— *Woodnotes*, II., p. 140.

GAME. Too long the g. is played.— *S. of Nat.*, p. 161.

GARDEN. Waters that wash my g. side.— *My Garden*, p. 174.

GENERATIVE. Miracle of g. force.— *Muske-taq.*, p. 166.

GEM. As the best g. upon her zone.— *The Problem*, p. 15.

GENESIS. Sweet the g. of things.— *Wood-notes*, II., p. 133.

GERMAN'S. G. inward sight.— *Monadnock*, p. 151.

GIBBOUS. G. moon.— *S. of Nat.*, p. 159.

GIRDS. G. the world with bound and term. — *I. D. and C. Love*, p. 108.

GLORY. With firmer g. fell.— *S. of Nat.*, p. 159.

GOBLIN. Musketaquit, a g. strong. — *Two Rivers*, p. 156.

GODS. Shadows flitting up and down. —*I. D. and C. Love*, p. 109.

 Delight in g.—*World-Soul*, p. 27.

 Speak it firmly, these are g.

 All are ghosts beside.—*Voluntaries*, p. 213.

 It whispers of the glorious g.—*World-Soul*, p. 25.

 The strong g. pine for my abode.—*Brahma*, p. 73.

GODHEAD. From world to world the g. changes.—*Woodnotes*, II., p. 139.

GOOD-BYE. G.-b. proud world. [Not reprinted in the final (1876) edition.]

GRACE. So sweet to Seyd as only g.—*Beauty*, p. 178.

GRANDEUR. So nigh is g. to our dust.—*Voluntaries*, p. 211.

GRANITE. Through the g. seeming.—*Monadnock*, p. 149.

GRASS. Poor g. shall plot and plan.—*Bacchus*, p. 118.

GREETING. Need is none of forms of g.—*I. D. and C. Love*, p. 110.

GRIM. G., gray rounding.—*Monadnock*, p. 152.

GROUND-PINE. G.-p. curled its pretty wreath.
—*Each and All*, p. 13.

GULF. G. of space.—*S. of Nat.*, p. 159.

GYPSY. G. beauty blazes higher.—*Romany Girl*, p. 86.

HALF-GODS. When h.-g. go.—*Give All to Love*, p. 85.

HALTETH. H. never in one shape.—*Woodnotes*, II., p. 139.

HARBINGER. Rainbow smiles his h.—*S. of Nat.*, p. 160.

HARP. Thy trivial h.—*Merlin*, p. 114.

HEARKEN. H.! h.! if thou wouldst know.—*Woodnotes*, II., p. 133.

HEAT. Hither rolls the storm of h.— *May-Day*, p. 44.

So pours the deluge of the h.
Broad northward o'er the land.—*May-Day*, p. 47.
What god is this imperial h.—*May-Day*, p. 45.

HEAVEN. Find me and turn thy back on H. —*Brahma*, p. 73.

Already H. with thee its lot has cast.—*Sursum Corda*, p. 79.

HIGHER. H. far into the pure realm.—*I. D. and C. Love*, p. 108.

HOLY GHOST. One accent of the H. G.— *The Problem*, p. 16.

HONEY. Like fiery h. sucked from roses.— *I. D. and C. Love*, p. 99.

    H. cloy.—*Waldeinsamkeit*, p. 157.

HOST. Girds with one flame the countless h. — *The Problem*, p. 15.

HOUR. Spirit strikes the h.— *Threnody*, p. 197.

HOUSE. We love the venerable h.—*Hymn*, p. 200.

HURL. H. wrong-doers down.— *Worship*, p. 183.

HYSON. One scent to h.—*Xenophanes*, p. 163.

IDEAS. Divine I. below.— *Ode to Beauty*, p. 82.

IMAGE. Molded an i.—*S. of Nat.*, p. 161.

IMPROVISATION. A divine i.— *Woodnotes*, II., p. 138.

INN. I. where he lodges for a night.— *Wood-notes*, II., p. 140.

INSIGHT.   To i. profounder.—*Sphinx*, p. 10.

INUNDATION.   I hear the i. sweet.— *Two Rivers*, p. 156.

JOVE.   Walks in mask almighty J.?—*May-Day*, p. 45

J. who deaf to prayers.—*Worship*, p. 183.

JUDÆAN.   In a J. manger.—*S. of Nat.*, p. 161.

JUSTICE.   J. conquers evermore.— *Voluntaries*, p. 212.

See *Voluntaries*, p. 213.

For there's no sequestered grot,
Lone mountain tarn, or isle forgot,
But J. journeying in her sphere,
Daily stoops to harbor there.—*Astræa*, p. 75.

KEEP.   And always k. us so. — *Ode to Beauty*, p. 82.

KING.   Conscious Law is k. of kings.— *Woodnotes*, II., p. 139.

KINGS.   God said, I am tired of k.—*Bost. Hymn*, p. 203.

KITE.   This treacherous k.—*Monadnock*, p. 152.

L AKE. Smote the l.—*Beauty*, p. 178.

LAUGHTER. L. rich as woodland thunder.— *Threnody*, p. 197.

LAVISH. L., l. promiser.—*Ode to Beauty*, p. 80.

LAYERS. Baked the l.—*S. of Nat.*, p. 160.

LEGS. Among the l. of his guardians tall.— *Experience*, p. 169.

LIBERTY. Found l. true l.—*Musketaq.*, p. 166.

LIGHT. Through l., through life. — *Two Rivers*.

LIKE. L. and unlike.—*Experience*, p. 169.

LILIES. A bunch of fragrant l. be.—*Woodnotes*, II., p. 140.

LION. Love laughs, and on a l. rides.—*I. D. and C. Love*, p. 105.

LITANIES. L. of nations came.—*The Problem* p. 14.

LORDS. The dear dangerous l.—*Musketaq.*, p. 164.
L. of life.—*Experience*, p. 169.

LORE. L. of colors and of sound.—*Musketaq.*, p. 166.

LOVE. Deep l. lieth under
These pictures of time.—*Sphinx*, p. 9.

LOVER. L. rooted stays.—*Friendship*, p. 177.
Have I a l. who is noble and free?—*The
Sphinx*, p. 10.

LOW. L. and mournful be the strain.—*Voluntaries*, p. 209.

MAN–CHILD. The m.-c. glorious.—*S. of
Nat.*, p. 160.

MAPLE-KEYS. The scarlet m.-k. betray.—
May-Day, p. 44.

MAPLE-JUICE. Drain sweet m.-j. in vats.—
Monadnock, p. 145.

MARL. Granite m. and shell.—*S. of Nat.*, p.
160.

MASK. Merry is only a m. of sad.—*Waldein-
samkeit*, p. 157.

MASTER. The passive M.—*The Problem*, p.
15.

MATTER. Build in m. home for mind.—
Wealth, p. 170.

MEAN. It was not for the m.—*Give all to
Love*, p. 84.

MEANINGS. Their noble m. are their pawns.
—*I. D. and C. Love*, p. 110.

MELIORATING. M. stars.—*S. of Nat.*, p. 159.

MELODY. A m. born of m.—*Fate*, p. 88.

MEMORIES. Smacks of m. far away.—*May-Day*, p. 42.

MERRY. M. is only a mask of sad.—*Waldein-samkeit*, p. 157.

METAMORPHOSIS. The rushing m.—*Wood-notes*, II., p. 133.

MILL-ROUND. M.-r. of our fate.—*Friendship*, p. 177.

MILLION-HANDED. The m.-h. painter pours.
—*May-Day*, p. 47.

MIND. And his m. is the sky,
 Than all it holds more deep, more high.—
 Woodnotes, II., p. 140.

MINE. M. are the night and morning.—*S. of Nat.*, p. 159.

MINIATURE. In soft m. lies.—*Sphinx*, p. 8.

MIRE. Leaves us in the m.—*World-Soul*, p. 25.

MISERIES. Our insect m.—*Monadnock*, p. 153.

MIX. M. the bowl again.—*S. of Nat.* p. 162.

MOAN. And joy and m.
Melt into one.—*I. D. and C. Love*, p. 108.

MOANINGS. M. of the tropic sea.—*Voluntaries*, p. 209.

MONADNOCK. She stood M.'s head.—*The Sphinx*, p. 11.

MORN. Painting with m.—*Problem*, p. 15.

MOURNFUL. M. be the strain.—*Voluntaries*, p. 209.

MUSIC. Who heard the starry m.—*Ode to Beauty*, p. 82.
M. pours on mortals.—*World-Soul*, p. 25.

MUSKETAQUIT. Thy summer voice, M.—*Two Rivers*, p. 156.

NAIL. N. the wild-star to its track.—*Threnody*, p. 198.

NAPHTHA. Flowed with n. fiery sweet.—*I. D. and C. Love*, p. 107.

NATURE. Him by the hand dear N. took.—*Experience*, p. 169.
Out from the heart of n. rolled.—*The Problem*, p. 14.
Universal N. through.—*Xenophanes*, p. 163.

NEW HAMPSHIRE. To the uplands of N. H. —*World-Soul*, p. 24.

NEVADA. N. coin thy golden crags.—*Bost. Hymn*, p. 206.

NILE. One over against the mouths of N.— *S. of Nat.*, p. 161.

NOBILITY. N. more nobly to repay.—*Forbearance*, p. 77.

NOBLE. I will have never a n.—*Bost. Hymn*, p. 204.

NYMPHS. Shun him, n., on the fleet horses!— *I. D. and C. Love*, p. 100.

OLD. Time to be o.—*Terminus*, p. 186.
OLYMPIAN. O. bards who sung
Divine Ideas below.—*Ode to Beauty*, p. 82.

OMENS. The youth reads o.—*May-Day*, p. 42.

OMNIPRESENT. O. without name.—*Experience*, p. 169.

ONWARD. Right o. drive unharmed.—*Terminus*, p. 187.

OPAL-COLORED. O.-c. days.—*May-Day*, p. 55.

8

OPTION. By fate, not o.—*Xenophanes*, p. 163.

OPULENT. O. soul, mingled from the generous whole.—*Ode to Beauty*, p. 81.

ORCHIS. Where in far fields the o. grew.—*Woodnotes*, I., p. 127.

ORGAN. The silent o. loudest chants.—*Dirge*, p. 189.

PADDLE. Or dip thy p. in the lake.—*Woodnotes*, II., p. 135.

PÆAN. Aloft, abroad the p. swells.—*Woodnotes*, II., p. 133.

PALLID. Thousand p. towns.—*May-Day*, p. 47.

PAN. Onward and on, the eternal P.—*Woodnotes*, II., p. 139.

PARADISE. The point is P. where their glances meet.—*I. D. and C. Love*, p. 107.

PAROQUET. An infinite p., Repeats one note. —*Xenophanes*, p. 163.

PARTHENON. Earth proudly wears the P.—*The Problem*, p. 15.

PAST. P., Present, Future shoot.—*I. D. and C. Love*, p. 108.

PEBBLE. Shining p. of the pond.— *Ode to Beauty*, p. 81.

PEBBLES. Flung in p. well to hear.— *Beauty*, p. 178.

PENTECOST. And ever the fiery P.— *The Problem*, p. 14.

PEREMPTORY. Free, p., clear.— *Merlin*, p. 114.

PERMANENCE. Type of p.— *Monadnock*, p. 153.

PIANO. Tinkle of p. strings.— *Merlin*, p. 114.

PICTURE. All was p. as he passed.— *Humblebee*, p. 60.

PICTURES. These p. of time.— *The Sphinx*, p. 9.

PINE. I that to-day am a p.— *Woodnotes*, II., p. 139.

PINE-TREE. So waved the p.-t. through my thought.— *Woodnotes*, II., p. 130.

PITS. P. of woe.— *Beauty*, p. 178.
P. of air.— *S. of Nat.*, p. 159.

PLAIN-DEALING. P.-d. nature gave.— *Musketaq.*, p. 166.

PLUMULE. Fled the last p. of the dark.— *Monadnock*, p. 151.

ROAD. Love delights to build a r.—*I. D. and C. Love*, p. 105.

ROBE. R. of snow.—*S. of Nat.*, p. 161.

ROMANCE. Grace and glimmer of r.—*Art*, p. 181.

ROSE. Speaks all languages the r.—*May-Day*, p. 43.

Through thee the r.—*Friendship*, p. 177.
Fresh r. on yonder thorn.—*S. of Nat.*, p. 162.

ROUNDING. Grim, gray r.—*Monadnock*, p. 152.

ROUTINE. Smug r.—*Mithridates*, p. 33.

RUDDER. Man the r.—*Terminus*, p. 187.

RUDDY. R. drop of manly blood.—*Friendship*, p. 177.

SAILING. S. through stars with all their history.—*Monadnock*, p. 150.

SALVE. S. my worst wounds.—*Musketaq.*, p. 166.

SANDS. S. whereof I'm made.—*Ode to Beauty*, p. 81.

SANNUP. *Musketaq.*, p. 165.

SCORNFUL. And his eye is s.,
  Threatening, and young.—*Fate*, p. 89.

SCOWL. I s. on him with my cloud.—*Monad-nock*, p. 152.

SCROLL. Rock and fire the s.—*S. of Nat.*, p. 160.

SEA-SAND. And one of the salt s.-s.—*S. of Nat.*, p. 161.

SECRET-SIGHT. As if by s.-s. he knew.—*Woodnotes*, I., p. 127.

SEER. Forest s.—*Woodnotes*, I., p. 127.

SEEMED. It seemed that Nature could not raise.—*Woodnotes*, I., p. 127.

SEEMING-SOLID. S.-s walls of use.—*Bacchus*, p. 118.

SEETHE. S., Fate! the ancient elements.—*S. of Nat.*, p. 162.

SERVETH. He that feeds men s. few.—*I. D. and C. Love*, p. 111.

SEVEN. Pine in vain the sacred S.—*Brahma*, p. 73.

SHAMS. I tire of s., I rush to Be.—*Nun's Aspiration*, p. 185.

SHARD. Of s. and flint makes pebbles gay.—*Two Rivers*, p. 156.

SHEEP. As s. go feeding in the waste.—*Woodnotes*, II., p. 139.

SHELL. Masters of the s.—*Ode to Beauty*, p. 82.

SHUDDERED. Cold s. the sphere.—*Sphinx*, p. 9.

SILVER. S. to s. creep and wind.—*I. D. and C. Love*, p. 109.
S. hills of heaven.—*Bacchus*, p. 117.

SIN. S. piles the loaded board.—*Woodnotes*, II., p. 130.

SINCERITY. Wrought in a sad s.—*Problem*, p. 14.

SKY. Through thee alone the s. is arched.—*Friendship*, p. 177.

SLAVE. The s. is owner, and ever was.—*Bost. Hymn*, p. 206.

SLAYER. If the red s. think he slays.—*Brahma*, p. 73.

SLIME. Flood's subsiding s.—*Woodnotes*, II., p. 133.

SLOWSURE. S. Britain's secular might.—*Monadnock*, p. 151.

SLUMBER. In s. I am strong.—*S. of Nat.*, p. 159.

SOBER. S. on a fund of joy.—*Waldeinsamkeit*, p. 157.

SOLAR. Secrets of the s. track.—*Merlin*, p. 114.

I bide in the s. glory.—*S. of Nat.*, p. 159.

SPADE. All my hurts my garden s. can heal. —*Musketaq.*, p. 166.

SPARKLE. He is the s. of the spar.—*Woodnotes*, II., p. 140.

SPELLS. The world is the ring of his s.— *Woodnotes*, II., p. 139.

SPENDING. I hear the s. of the stream.—*Two Rivers*, p. 156.

SPENT. S. and aged things.—*S. of Nat.*, p. 160.

SPHINX. Uprose the merry s.—*Sphinx*, p. 11.

SPIDERS. Swinging s. silver line.—*Ode to Beauty*, p. 81.

SPILLING. S. over the mountain-chains.— *May-Day*, p. 47.

SPIRES. Through all the s. of form.—*May-Day*, p. 42.

SPORTIVE. S. sun.—*S. of Nat.*, p. 159.

SPRING. Daughter of Heaven and Earth, coy S.—*May-Day*, p. 41.

SPRUCE. Pants up hither the s. clerk.—*Monadnock*, p. 151.

STAFF. Wave thy s. in air.—*Woodnotes*, p. 135.

STAINLESS. S. soldier on the walls.—*Voluntaries*, p. 212.

STAR-DUST. S.-d. and star pilgrimages.—*Woodnotes*, II., p. 133.

STAR-FORM. Why the s.-f. she repeats.—*Woodnotes*, p. 127.

STARS. Fetch her s. to deck her hair.—*To Rhea*, p. 22.

STREAM. Dark s. that seaward creeps.—*Conc. Fight*, p. 202.

    The s. I love unbounded goes.—*Two Rivers*, p. 156.

SUBSTANCES. S. at base divided.—*I. D. and C. Love*, p. 108.

SUCCESSION. S. swift.—*Experience*, p. 169.

SUCCORY. S. to match the sky.—*Humblebee*, p. 60.

SUN. Will take the s. out of the skies.—*Ode*, p. 208.

    The s. himself shines heartily.—*World-Soul*, p. 26.

SUN-BAKED. Singing in the s.-b square.—
Art, p. 181.

SUNBURNT. S. world a man shall breed.—
S. of Nat., p. 162.

SUN-PATH. S.-p. in thy worth.—*Friendship*,
p. 177.

SUPERSOLAR. Sparks of the s. blaze.—*Merlin*, p. 114.

SURFACE. S. and Dream.—*Experience*, p.
169.

SURGE. S. of summer's beauty.—*Musketaq.*,
p. 164.

SURGING. S. sea outweighs.—*Friendship*, p.
177.

SURPRISE. Stair-way of s.—*Merlin*, p. 115.

SURVEYORS. Time and Thought were my s.
—*S. of Nat.*, p. 160.

SWATHED. S. their too much power.—*S. of
Nat.*, p. 160.

SWORD. Masters the s.—*Fate*, p. 89.

SYNOD. Airy s. bends.—*I. D. and C. Love*,
p. 103.

TALLIES. Counted my t.—*S. of Nat.*, p. 159.

TAP-ROOTS. T.-r. reaching through under the Andes.—*Bacchus*, p. 117.

TAYLOR. T., the Shakespeare of divines.— *The Problem*, p. 16.

TEEM. T. with unwonted thoughts.—*I. D. and C. Love*, p. 103.

TENDENCY. T. through endless ages.—*Wood-notes*, II., p. 133.

TENDERLY. T. the haughty day.—*Ode*, p. 207.

TENEMENTS. Innumerable t. of beauty.— *Musketaq.*, p. 166.

TENSE. Affirmer of the present t.—*Monadnock*, p. 153.

THANKS. T. to the morning light.—*World-Soul*, p. 24.

THATCH. T. with towns the prairie broad.— *World-Soul*, p. 26.

THOUGHT'S. T. perilous, whirling pool.— *Threnody*, p. 197.

Out of T. interior sphere.—*The Problem*, p. 15.

T. causing stream.—*World-Soul,* p. 26.

THREADING. T. dark ways, arriving late.—
Worship, p. 183.

THROB. This mound shall t.—*Monadnock*,
p. 150.

TIDE. Time and t. forever run.—*S. of Nat.*,
p. 161.

TINTS. Refresh the faded t.—*Bacchus*, p.
119.

TIRE. T. of globes and races.—*S. of Nat.*,
p. 161.

TORRENT. Rest on the pitch of the t.—*S. of
Nat.*, p. 159.

TORRENTS. Wine that is shed
  Like the t. of the sun
  Up the horizon walls.—*Bacchus*, p. 118.

TOWN-SPRINKLED. T.-s. lands that be.—
Monadnock, p. 150.

TRAILS. To hunt upon their shining t.—
Forerunners, p. 68.

TRANSPARENCY. He hides in pure t.—*Woodnotes*, II., p. 140.

TRAVAIL. T. in pain for him.—*S. of Nat.*,
p. 161.

TRIBES. T. my house can fill.—*S. of Nat.*,
p. 159.

TROUBADOUR. Comes that cheerful T.—
Monadnock, p. 150.

TRUE. He serves all who dares to be t.— *I.
D. and C. Love*, p. 111.

TUMBLING. T. steep in the uncontinented
deep.—*Monadnock*, p. 152.

TUNE. Nature beats in perfect t.—*Woodnotes*,
II., p. 135.

TWICE. T. I have molded an image.—*S. of
Nat.*, p. 161.

UNCONTINENTED. U. deep.—*Monadnock*, p. 152.

UNIVERSE. Beam to the bounds of the u.—
Beauty, p. 178.

UNKNOWN. Known fruit of the u.—*Sphinx*,
p. 7.

UNMAKE. U. me quite.—*Ode to Beauty*, p.
81.

UNTAUGHT STRAIN. You must add the u. s.
—*Fate*, p. 88.

URN. Fills his blue u. with fire.—*Ode*, p. 207.

USE. U. and surprise.—*Experience*, p. 169.

VAN. On thy broad mystic v.—*May-Day*, p. 55.

VAULT. This v. which glows immense.— *Woodnotes*, II., p. 140.

VEGETABLE GOLD.— *Guy*, p. 91.

VICTIM. V. lying low.—*Voluntaries*, p. 212.

VOICES. Through a thousand v.—*Sphinx*, p. 11.

WEB. Play not in Nature's lawful w.— *My Garden*, p. 174.

WHEEL. In a region where the w.—*I. D. and C. Love*, p. 108.

WHEELS. W. which whirl the sun.—*S. of Nat.*, p. 161.

WHIRL. W. the glowing wheels.—*S. of Nat.*, p. 162.

WHOLE. The linked purpose of the w.— *Musketaq.*, p. 166.

I yielded myself to the perfect w.—*Each and All*, p. 13.

WINGS. I am the w.— *Brahma*, p. 73.

WINE. Pouring of his power the w.—*Woodnotes*, II., p. 139.

WOODGODS. The partial w.—*Musketaq.*, p. 164.

WOOD-ROSE. Loved the w.-r. and left it on its stalk.—*Forbearance*, p. 77.

WOODS. W. at heart are glad.—*Waldein-samkeit*, p. 157.

WORKETH. W. high and wise.—*Ode*, p. 208.

WORLD. W. rolls round, mistrust it not.—*May-Day*, p. 47.

WORM. Starred eternal w.—*I. D. and C. Love*, p. 108.
　　Striving to be man, the w.—*May-Day*, p. 42.

WORSE. Alike to him the better, the w.—*Woodnotes*, II., p. 140.

WREATH. W. shall nothing miss.—*S. of Nat.*, p. 159.

WRITE. W. the past in characters.—*S. of Nat.*, p. 160.

YAWNS. Y. the pit of the Dragon.—*Sphinx*, p. 9.

YELLOW-BREECHED. Y.-b. philosopher.—*Humblebee*, p. 60.

YOUNG. Always find us y.—*Ode to Beauty*, p. 82.

YOUTH. Y. replies, *I can.—Voluntaries*, p. 211.

ZODIAC. On the half-climbed z.—*Threnody*, p. 198.

ZONES. Of all the z. and countless days.—*S. of Nat.*, p. 162.

EMERSON
AS A MAGAZINE TOPIC.

THE following list of magazine and periodical essays upon Emerson was — for the most part — contributed to the *Chicago Dial*, by Mr. Poole, from his new "Index to Periodical Literature," and we have permission to use it here. But we have found it necessary to append a number of recent titles, to bring the list down to our present date:

Emerson, Ralph Waldo (R. Buchanan), Broadway,
   2 : 223.—(J. Burroughs) Galaxy, 21 : 254, 543.
   —(D. M. Colton) Continental Monthly, 1 :
   49.—(G. Gilfillan) Tait's Magazine, *n. s.*, 15 :
   17. Same article, Living Age, 16 : 97.—(J.
   O'Connor) Catholic World, 27 : 90.—(G. Prentice) Methodist Quarterly, 24 : 357.—Dublin
   Review, 26 : 152.—North British Review, 47 :

319.—Westminster Review, 33: 345.—Black-
wood, 62: 643.—(F. H. Underwood) North
American Review, 130: 479.—(B. Herford)
Dial (Ch.), 2: 114.

—— Address, July, 1838. Boston Quarterly, 1:
500.

—— Address on Forefathers' Day, 1870. (I. N.
Tarbox) New Englander, 30: 175.

—— and his writings (G. Barmby). Howitt's Journal, 2: 315.—Christian Review, 26: 640.

—— and History. Southern Literary Messenger,
18: 249.

—— and Landor. Living Age, 52: 371.

—— and the Pantheists (H. Hemming). New Do-
minion, 8: 65.

—— and Transcendentalism. American Whig Review, 1: 233. See *Transcendentalism*.

—— and Spencer and Martineau. (W. R. Alger)
Christian Examiner, 84: 257.

—— Conduct of Life. (N. Porter) New Englander,
19: 496.—Eclectic Review, 46: 365.

—— Culture. Fraser, 78: 1. Same art., Living
Age, 98: 358.

—— English Traits. See *England*.

—— Essays. Democratic Review, 16: 589.—Eclectic Magazine, 18: 546.—Living Age, 4: 139;
23: 344.—(C. C. Felton) Christian Examiner,
30: 253.—Eclectic Review, 76: 667.—Boston
Quarterly, 4: 391.—Biblical Review, 1: 148.—

Prospective Review, 1 : 232.— Tait's Magazine
n. s., 8: 666.
—— Home and Haunts of. (F. B. Sanborn) Scrib-
ner, 17: 496.
—— Lectures at Manchester. Howitt's Journal, 2 :
370.
—— Visit to Scotland. Douglas Jerrold's Shilling
Magazine, April, 1848.
—— Lectures and Writings of. Every Saturday, 3 :
680 ; 4: 381.
—— Letters and Social Aims. International Re-
view, 3 : 249.
—— New Lectures. Christian Review, 15 : 249.
—— Poems. (C. E. Norton) Nation, 4 : 430.—
American Whig Review, 6 : 197.—(C. A. Bar-
tol) Christian Examiner, 42 : 255.— Southern
Literary Messenger, 13 : 292.— Brownson, 4 :
262.— Democratic Review, 1 : 319.— Christian
Remembrancer, 15 : 300.
—— Prose Works. Catholic World, 11 : 202.
—— Recent Lectures and Writings. Fraser, 75 :
586. Same article, Living Age, 93 : 581.
—— Representative Men. (C. A. Bartol) Christian
Examiner, 48 : 314.— Eclectic Review, 95 : 568.
— British Quarterly, 11 : 281.
—— Society and Solitude. Fraser, 82 : 1.—(D.
March) New Englander, 8 : 186.
—— Writings. (F. H. Hedge) Christian Examiner,
38 : 87.—(J. W. Alexander) Princeton Review,
13 : 539.

—— Chambers's Journal, 21, 382.
—— Emerson number of Boston Literary World, May, 1881.
—— North American Review, July, 1882.
—— Lippincott's Magazine, November, 1882.
—— Atlantic Monthly, August, 1882.
—— Harpers' Monthly, July and September, 1882.
—— Baldwin's Monthly, December, 1881.
—— Demorest's Monthly, July, 1882.
—— Harpers' Weekly, June 10, 1882.
—— The Century, July, 1882.
—— The Modern Review, October, 1882.
—— Fortnightly Review, June, 1882.
—— London Illustrated News, May 6, 1882.
—— London Graphic, May 6, 1882.
—— London Athenæum, May 6, 1882.
—— London Academy, May 6, 1882.
—— Gentleman's Magazine, November, 1882.
—— Colburn's New Monthly Magazine, December, 1882.

Various articles upon Emerson have also appeared in French, German, and other continental magazines; but, as we cannot command the dates necessary to make an account of them reasonably complete, we forego the attempt.